Shake the Kaleidoscope

G W Colkitto

Cinnamon Press
:: small miracles from distinctive voices ::

Published by Cinnamon Press
www.cinnamonpress.com

The right of G W Colkitto to be identified as author of this work has been asserted by him in accordance with the Copyright, Designs and Patent Act, 1988. © 2022, G W Colkitto
ISBN 978-1-78864-146-3

British Library Cataloguing in Publication Data. A CIP record for this book can be obtained from the British Library.

All rights reserved. No part of this publication may be reproduced, stored in a retrieval system, or transmitted in any form or by any means, electronic, mechanical, photocopying, recording or otherwise without the prior written permission of the publishers. This book may not be lent, hired out, resold or otherwise disposed of by way of trade in any form of binding or cover other than that in which it is published, without the prior consent of the publishers.

Designed and typeset in Bodoni by Cinnamon Press. Cover design by Adam Craig © Adam Craig.

Cinnamon Press is represented by Inpress.

Acknowledgements

This collection would not have been possible without the support of my friends, Mo Blake, Ian and Linda Hunter, Wullie Purcell, and Finola Scott. I am also deeply indebted to the advice of Jen Hadfield and John Glenday, tutors on my first visit to Moniack Mhor, and to many subsequent tutors. I have been fortunate to call on the knowledge and encouragement of Dr Sally Evans. Finally, I have benefited greatly from Cinnamon Courses in Wales and on-line. The idea for this collection came from conversations with Jan Fortune. It is a joy to work with Jan and with all at Cinnamon Press.

Poetry is my Kaleidoscope. Every day brings fragments of light and time which create images I try to capture. A glimpse of emotion which no matter how fleeting has an impact, just as those patterns of shimmer and colour entranced me as a child. These poems are (in the main) randomly shaken from my attempts to hold in words those images of time and chance. I hope like the Kaleidoscope they draw you in.

Contents

Year 14: For love of what…	9
Year 22: Chaff	10
Year 63: An Orkney Prayer	11
Year 12: A religious man curses	12
Year 17: The Scots Pine	13
Year 63: The Poet makes notes	14
Year 5: In a tenement house 1954	15
Year 33: A coo twa goats an a dug	16
Year 19: Spellbound	17
Year 31: A Death in the Family	18
Year 64: They sold me flowers	19
Year 60: Elegy in a Johnstone garden	20
Year 57: For Love—Oh God	21
Year 62: Shopping Maul	22
Year 35: Animal Farm	23
Year 20: Echo of the night	24
Year 58: Footsteps on the Beach	25
Year 57: Banana and bacon trifle	26
Year 41: Café—Bowness on Windermere	27
Year 45: Perceptions of Cruelty	28
Year 60: When memories sing the sadness of hotels in their degeneration	30
Year 72: Children of Another God	31
Year 31: Nor man's empty praise	32
Year 24: Back Street Fashion	33
Year 69: Are we there yet?	34
Year 20: Soul Singer	36
Year 70: As I sip Pinot Grigio	37
Year 26: Ode to a Candle	38
Year 7: Day trips with Dad	39
Year 69: At Parkhill Wood	40
Year 3: The Hut	41
Year 70: A Glasgow Hug	42
Year 4: I called him dad, but what's in a name	43
Year 67: Bird Throng	44
Year 2: Worm	45
Year 55: mining silver coins on Coniston	46
Year 8: No blue plaque	47
Year 72: Desiderata—out of Covid desolation	48
Year 72: When Edison found light	49
Year 7: My Earth is Flat	50
Year 25: Thoughts on a brown gown	51
Year 46: Out-going tide	52

Year 33: To Sail Away	53
Year 3: A tortoise in a Parliament	54
Year 30: Worship in the Tabernacle—Corrie	55
Year 71: On the Final Journey of Wise Men	56
Year 30: Condemned by beauty	57
Year 48: Bamburgh Castle	58
Year 72: As if	60
Year 11: Nothing but a paper pusher	61
Year 57: Plasticine to Camembert	62
Year 19: Pub Faces—In All Her Glory	63
Year 27: Please mind the gap	64
Year 10: Nancy Pretty	65
Year 57: At Moniack—this landscape has not changed	66
Year 22: A Law unto Himself	67
Year 66: Agnes Burns—Song Book	68
Year 22: Into Heaven	69
Year 54: Edge of time	70
Year 23: Drive a Hillman Imp and you'll want to smile	72
Year 68: For Tammy and Robert— Wedding At Sherbrooke Castle Hotel	73
Year 9: Old Mrs Kerr	74
Year 51: Although that love was mine	76
Year 52: Blackbird in the Holly	77
Year 18: Right Up Tight	78
Year 68: Song for lost windows	79
Year 72: Playing with Truth	80
Year 61: When the trees move	82
Year 57: Lindisfarne	83
Year 50: The Question is…	84
Year 54: Miles to go before we sleep	85
Year 9: Standing Stones, Kingarth, Isle of Bute	86
Year 72: all the dogs died	88
Year 5: Glacé Fruits	89
Year 53: This door is not a means of escape	90
Year 16: Holiday Slides	91
Year 6: Walking toy	92
Year 24: Black Park, Tullochgrue	94
Year 66: hopeful of words	95
Year 9: Meditation on Kirkwall	96
Year 59: Thoughts in a spring garden	97
Year 63: Home to Orkney	98
Year 71: Here in the poets zoo	102

Shake the Kaleidoscope

Year 14

For love of what…

my first poem came in a dream

for love of what I could not be
I gave away my jollity
for hope of what I can become
I take it back it was such fun

Year 22

Chaff

I cannot speak my thoughts
they're so confused
like chaff out in a gale
I sit here in a dream
waiting till we meet again
and fear lest you should turn
and brush me off as dust
for this compared to you
indeed I am
but if you wish to break me in
I promise to be less recalcitrant
than the wayward horse
and take with joy
the bounty of your smile
so spur me if you will
but spurn me not
for I too may try to jump
so high a gate in dire despair
in hope that you will come
and comfort me

Year 63

An Orkney Prayer

like some old ceremony conducted by priests we have been gathered
from many parts drunk together talked as strangers
have become friends
I could run on with this and have a feeling
in these circling thoughts
(clockwise never widdershins)
each came our own stone
with names scratched into us
with dates   with broken parts
from lightening strikes
from unseen blows
by others
or self inflicted

chipped and aged
we sit in a ring
voices I hear voices
I hear
                 i

and now not i
some indefinable shift in soul
in those voices
spoken imagined embracing loving
an incantation
Trust   your self
Trust   your reader
Trust   your listener
 and as I chant   an inner whisper
Trust   your fellow poets.
I am crying
—maybe I should not tell you that—but I trust you
run your lips through my tears

Year 12

A religious man curses

the coffin arrives on the start
of his journey from home
the room in dead silence
even air hangs lifeless

I fight to see   faces
draw back   these are
heartless   cold   dim
this Brethren funeral
soulless   no hand
reaches out

no word to hold   my
tight strangled need
to cry   is swallowed
I shrink   behind settee
too young for a place
near the body   too young
for a seat   too old for
a smile

The preacher's voice   a dirge
in this room where I laughed
and felt the warmth   once
wrapped by   the corpse

the room fades   fades   slips
I become another unconscious
in mourning   become distraction
from the preacher's God   so that
reviving water   brought for the child
has a chill   a biblical curse   I see
how vampire like he hangs   over
all   how deeply he hates   me
clinging   to life

Year 17

The Scots Pine

first published poem—Glasgow Herald

Lonely on a hillside
stark and gaunt
a Scots pine stands
sentinel of want

dominates the moorland
dreich and grey
bent for ever
the windy way

am I the Scots pine
on the hill
and it a person
standing there so still

Year 63

The Poet makes notes

In the whisky bar of the Stromness Hotel,
listening to the insignificances,
as the numbers dwindle,
until the hard-core late drinkers sit,
malts spread around,
a half-comatose head lifts to say
'OK lass' to an imagined companion,
drinks, slumps asleep.
A man with no teeth mumbles,
—of loneliness, of the empty home,
orders another double,
filling the emptiness.
The poet makes notes

Year 5

In a tenement house 1954

Dark brown stained
wood entrapped in church varnish
dust laden curtains barely parted
A single ray of day slips in
the brass plaque above the mantle reflects
sending the light to die in the frozen room
Lace antimacassars isolated white
on dark flower embroidery chairs
catch the ending and black shadows leap
from scatter cushions to mock the sleeping cat
A spark floats lazily up the chimney
last ember of a dying fire

There is a figure sinking in one chair
as grey as the room
fading from view, from the light
waiting for the passing into night

Year 33

A coo twa goats an a dug

Folk aye speir at a bairn
'whit will ye be when yer a man?'

Me - aa wantit tae be a fairmer
Nae a muckle fairm wi mony beasts
aa dinna fancy aw the trackle
juist a bittie hous an a coo
twa goats an a dug

Aa wis bit a laddie
hoo wis aa tae ken life isnae fer dreams
ye hae tae guddle alang wi the cairds yer delt

Sae aa became an accoontant
wi an office an twa worries
siller gien in an sillar gien oot

Oan a Seturday awa frae the hale clamjafrey
aa culd saunter by the river
tak oan a wis a fairmer oan ma ain land
ben an glen belanged tae me

Oan a Monday the hale whigmaleerie
wis back in the press wi the wax jaiket
aa wis anither peerie
spinnin in the stream o dreich drudgery.

Year 19

Spellbound

Here is the magic of a million years
bound up in one
a single smile and the will avers
that I am won

the mind runs on
but the balance is disturbed
for half goes off
no
more than half
with you

one glance
one friendly word
and I am yours
I fly so high
higher than I know
I fear to fall
and yet
I like it so

and yet I feel
unworthy as I am
that you may scorn my praise
and turn away from this most wretched muse
and leave him
still within your spell
with sorrow in his heart
to worship from afar

Year 31

A Death in the Family

The street is filling with cars,
solemn women in shapeless black,
grim men stiff as the white shirt.

Here a group gather, shake hands,
smile quiet smiles, little nods of recognition,
small shrugs of sympathy.

A car door slams and heads jerk
throwing glances at the thoughtlessness,
at the face they cannot place.

Wedding and Christening did not bring all these,
the cobweb tendrils of blood and time.

For some this is a rehearsal for the funeral
they will not see. A check on numbers,
as if quantity absolves the life, proves the worth.

Others are passing briefly between demands of living,
thoughts half here, half in things interrupted.
All weigh each word, given and received.

Inside they wait in half light,
gathered in, girded for the day.
Watch history arriving to release

another broken link in the chain,
their anchor weaker.

Year 64

They sold me flowers

the scent of freesia
filling the room

sharp yellow of daffodil
in spring brightens the window

red roses six to speak of love
dark with passion spiked with pain

lilies dropping petals white
falling to lie round the hymnary

and now I have the empty vase
its crystal diamonds etched by winter sun
rainbow colours prismed on the table

Year 60

Elegy in a Johnstone garden

tonight a breeze speaks softly and alone
beneath a vault of leaves as in a church
a psalm begins to gather and I groan
whisp'ring of love to the silver birch

trees seem to move as I embrace the moon
delight as pipistrelles like ancient ghosts
come to flit the void and the darkling town
recedes as I remember inky coasts

waves rolling home to fade on glinting sands
footprints filled and lost and made again
the way they came together a twisted band
when two were one then two then one that pain

—realising days and traces all must die
your face once clear is now like evening cloud
trailed beyond the limit of my eyes
under my feet snowdrops white and bowed

are crushed and broken as I wander here
this morning I picked others for our room
for these simple flowers—to you so dear
to me hold life and death in every bloom

Year 57

For Love—Oh God

Where is the blood that I have none to shed?
It lies congealed, frozen in the vein.
A struggling heart beats but all in vain,
it cannot move what has become as dead
as roses torn from the stem, a lily ground
beneath the heel. When icy winds blast
the barren slopes, tiny purple flowers last
among the withered stalks and their bells sound
that beauty will not die; but I am dead
within, though outwardly my body stands,
no sap rises, love dripping from these hands
turned poison. Nothing lives to lift its head,
no crimson poppy springs from where I die.
I thought that you were true and yet you lie.

Year 62

Shopping Maul

tis madden in the grumbly grew
shoppers in their spree and whirl
all girny gangly drubbly squirm
all hopely cashly lust and burst
dargy sons and surly daughters
slow low feet and highly straughters
tis after bought and disappointed
parcels juggled arms disjointed
tis madden in the jungly grew

winsom wenches aw aknowin
spotted yinyans macho strollin
grannies splot in heavy garb
mothers grizzle at sprogs sad greetin
bodgers sit eye them aw passin
churnin masses strach and strinnel
in maelstrom horde a runnin bairnie
shouts he needs tae find a lavvie
tis madden in the chungly grew

and sunny is the glassy under
slippy slidey feet asunder
senseless prattly grab and bunter
rushly bustly haste and brillsome
escaped from toil to bream and boil
in tempty mile shopkeepers frappy
tomorrows wages gone so snappy
jingly jangly till music ringin
tis madden in the fungly grew

Year 35

Animal Farm

the elephant has crapped on my tortoise
it did not move quickly enough
so now I am sifting through shit
piles of the stinking stuff

the kangaroo peed on my trousers
while I was crouching down here
thank god I am wearing galoshes
or I'd faint with the smell I fear

my bladder has emptied in panic
my bowels, they hang by a thread
if the tablets don't kick in as wanted
I may go out of my head

but the doctor has promised they'll save me
from the everything life may throw
and I trust his professional judgement
I'm an idiot as you know

you have to believe in something
when the ostrich sits on your head
for if you believe in nothing
you might as well be dead

Year 20

Echo of the night

There is a sad and simpered sound down in the alley
joined with deadest leaves about the gate
a late man in the street near-by
hurries homeward but not straight
glancing, like his ancestors, listening for their call

He hears this sound
a timeless spaceless echo of the night
and twists his head
but still he cannot tell if he is right
or is it just the darkness of his past

And all the time
the invisible cloak descends
and whiter teeth and eye now shine
and lower crouched the shadow wends
its course between the pillared lights

Thus as he opens the gate to home
the merest smirk about his mouth appears
for it is just the winds that moan
and tall his stride for nothing fears
and his cloak is firm about him

The swirling wind down in the alley
still turns the leaves against the gate
but no sound in the street near-by
is heard by man out walking late
and the cat which waited goes on by

Year 58

Footsteps on the Beach

Bamburgh

That time when all have left
the beach empty.
I walk, towards the Farnes,
under the castle.
More memories than waves breaking.

I came for this. A salty reuniting.
So real I look at the footsteps, disappointed
there is only one set.
In my mind I see the shape of your foot
and hear, in the breeze, your laugh.

I realise how much of me has died, and am surprised
my footprints are as deep as ever.
I step round jellyfish, which worried you,
but never bothered me before.
Now I cannot protect you from them
I have to protect me. A symbiosis
where I live for two,
having half died with one.

Year 57

Banana and bacon trifle

this is crazy food
a mere trifle gone bananas
rasher mouths mix their pleasures
make a pig of themselves
custard and bacon
like Rosencrantz and Guildenstern pretending
to be a sweet concoction

Year 41

Café—Bowness on Windermere

It is strange how often I recall that café
that afternoon memorable
two coffees and two buns

the lack of a view to lake or mountain
should have other cafés higher on my list
but there was comfort here with you
which fixed time and place

other cafés crowd in to make their claim
cinnamon toast in Hexham
scone teas in Alnwick
hot peas in The Ritz on Cumbrae

there are reasons for me to go back to them
locations   familiarity   a broken journey

Bowness was a short walk through the town
window browsing before going to our hotel
killing time with a Cappuccino
nothing to return for

except that feeling of certainty
when tomorrow was endless

Year 45

Perceptions of Cruelty

Lerwick Harbour 1959–Paisley 1994

Shaggy cattle mill in wooden pens
the quayside echoes with hoof and bellow

Dockers open a gate and the beasts
are pushed into a channel of hurdles
they move, bellow resistance, stop
stubbornly stiff-legged
at the wooden gangway
inches of metal skewer flashes
it plunges into hairy rump
the animal bucks and stumbles
roars as it charges the ramp
its sudden movement galvanises the others
soon all are corralled on board

This performance of resistance
fast stab
repeats pen by pen
until
in less than one hour
the dock is empty
on deck
cattle eat and chunter

I look down on them
impressed by the efficiency
stunned by the cruelty

Decades later I have to move one pig
the foolishness of a friend's pet
which has grown from cuddly to gross
turning garden into mud and neighbours
into enemies

We arrive with estate car
dock it on the path
construct alley way and ramp

Full of kindness and sensitivity
we coax the sow into the channel
it screams and cries twists and revolts
refuses to move up the rickety ramp.

We push with boards
it is immoveable.

We tempt with titbits
it screams disgust.

After hours of conflict, exhaustion defeats her
we force her into the car
which sags under her weight
she slumping on the estate bed

As the car leaves I see the sow
prostrate in the rear and wonder
if an old docker looks down
staggered by our inefficiency
stunned at our unseeing cruelty.

Year 60

When memories sing the sadness of hotels
in their degeneration

this is the cost of holidays
in roads and buildings and this
complex of concrete crushing
a dead landscape like a child
playing with toy buildings on
a coffin

this started as heather and gorse
where the eye was embraced by
the curve of distant mountain
pine forest then minor intrusion of
the first hotel where windows
mirrored purple and blue

now the hoards have bruised
and broken the bond between
hotel and the reason there was
a hotel so this is a living death
a body laid out and embalmed
so that the hot tubs and ice
rinks can pretend there is a
reason to be at one with the
corpse

Year 72

Children of Another God

when they dive to the forest of dead turbines

will they dig broken blades from sediments
Saying—*what technology gave these flight*

will they find a preserved Big Mac and puzzle
at its purpose

will they bring nebulisers to the surface wonder
if our lungs withered with the vegetation

when all is flood and desert
when all computers have lost memory

when all memory has
become myth

will they light fires and smoke dope
Sing—*If I was a rich man*

Year 31

Nor man's empty praise

He says 'people like these'
the other side of the table nods

                    I swallow a mouthful of dust

Fancy sauce and fillet of venison
the bright white teeth across acres of polish
spit out another certainty 'not willing to work'

the man who inherited
a name, an estate, a shipping line
the man who is tall

                    I hate his height, his teeth
                    people like him

                    I eat the meal
                    praise the careful wine
                    accept the whisky

same name as the small man who smiles
and owns this building

                    Do I hate him
                    not as much for
                    he is my height

but then he repeats 'People'
that separate race who grind the streets
below – 'These People, don't know they're born'

                    I rattle the silver spoon
                    in my coffee and stir in
                    sugars from Caribbean Plantations

                    swallow words that would cost
                    me my job
                    consider who pays

Year 24

Back Street Fashion

she carries High Fashion through flat suburbia
even on rainy Tuesdays her ice-blue turban
chiffon sparkle scarf constellation bright
floating behind as she streams past
as if on her way through Montmartre
Iceland is her Sacre-Coeur to check out
a Cordon Bleu meal for one a crisp white wine
tomorrow she will shine again her light
beaming on those who smile at her style

Year 69

Are we there yet?

we pack the SUV
pull away from our house

waters are rising

no need to check the electrics
everything we own is smart

rain is falling

we pass overflowing rainbow bins
we are not thoughtless discarders
but we have to be on trend – of today

waters are rising

we do not stick in mud
our garden is hard landscape
our artificial grass glistens like jewels

rain is falling

the bird-feeders stand forlorn
I remember thrush, blue-tit, wren,
no barrage of sparrows, no singing, as we leave

waters are rising

the children watch 'The Blue Planet'
ask if we saw an actual Dodo,
were our old days good?

rain is falling

is the flood a myth
those far off islands that drowned
fake news, to frighten the gullible?

waters are rising

it goes in cycles
ice age, drought, flood, we survive
don't we?

rain is falling

if we had listened
if we had understood
we might know where to go

the waters are rising

Year 20

Soul Singer

she is all bust and sashay
as she drops her shoulder
swings those hips
I am impaled on her breasts
her smile burning my eyes
flaming   flaming   flaming   woman
why did God make legs like hers

she struts over my longing
I roast in the fires of lust

woman you are gold and uranium
never tarnished and deadly
I mine those seams seeking treasure
knowing I will die a little
as I come to life

her indigo cords ensnare my heart
its beat quickens to her rhythm

Year 70

As I sip Pinot Grigio

They are under a Glasgow bridge, on the pavement
at the Heilan Man's Umbrella, with a bundle of little,

while I am sad in a comfortable room,
can afford heating, have a bed for the night,
sit with glass of anaesthetic wine.

When it is freezing piss in plastic bottles
I will tot up wealth on the laptop,
will worry about my legacy.

They will see the rain,
claim their place beneath Victorian cast iron,
ask revellers for loose change.

I beg you, explain.

But I can wait to understand
for there is wine in my glass
and I begin to feel nothing.

Year 26

Ode to a Candle

A burning symbol of romance
with kissing rays on lovers' face
that cause the smitten heart to dance
                              the eye to gaze

A flicker like the nearly dead
flame and shadow intertwined
in hint of smoke lie dreams unsaid
                              all in the mind

A simple glow throughout the years
has signaled hope in darkest night
better the smile, softer the tears
                              by candlelight

Year 7

Day trips with Dad

It was what he did when we went away for the day, made up sandwiches, egg, cold bacon. If we were being posh - salmon, a little bit of salad, lettuce, tomato, cucumber. It didn't matter how far we were going, he took a kettle -- a stove -- the kitchen sink, everything so that we wouldn't have to go in somewhere and pay exorbitant prices. We watched the fun, his excitement as he tried to light a Primus stove, in the wind and out in the rain, to make a cup of tea. Get a rug out of the car, spread over the wet grass, determined we would enjoy a picnic, despite dampness creeping up his legs, as he handed us our treats.

Year 69

At Parkhill Wood

high on purple blues we take the seldom path
drugged on evening scent
bluebell and hawthorn fill our lungs
a pink galaxy of campion catches the sun
we lose the names of white drifts
wonder whether we skirt comfrey or cowslip
careful not to crush their waiting yellow
we breath we live seeking pale blue
finding delicate curved stems
through the trees pastoral green leads us
pubwards to toast these memories
and as we leave as if on cue
herons returning to their nest
glide over the stand of dark firs
a cacophony of rooks rising
drowns our laughter

Year 3

The Hut

in this summer brightness
I am a pup again with Dad
outside the garden shed as he saws
to fix a step for me to mount
the rocking horse whose head he crafted
in the shed at his vice
whose eye he painted and whose reins
made of ribboned cord hang loose for me
the mane an old brown carpet strip
I watched him tack with care
and did not dare to say I hated how it felt
to me like cotton wool in Aspirin shiver
and baking in the sun I shiver as if
the future had come shadowed and adult
he smiles at my impatience holds out his hand
and I step up to his step

in the hut are his drawer of sharpened chisels
the carefully adjusted planes the line of lasts
from father down to me
leather wax and thread for him to repair shoes
I wear happily strike sparks from segs
click click my way into today.

Year 70

A Glasgow Hug

the city breathes in
he feels its hard edges
the surge of night streets

at the corner he swithers
routes home
wonders

how many are making tea
spoons clinking on saucers
how many in bed
curved in love

he is swallowed by a bear hug
swung from his feet
by a booze-happy man
who leans close

You remind me of ma Dad
He smiles, nods, feels the warmth
Ma Dad, the voice cracks
is in a hospice... dying

He watches the man roll on
swirling away in that tide of night
whose voices haunt him

lanes pull at his fears
dark fissures threatening
to suck him in

laughter echoes from somewhere
and he wishes it was his
sweet memories on his tongue

he wants to join the revellers
wants to belong

Year 4

I called him dad, but what's in a name

he called me Speugh
his little sparrow
as I chirruped round his feet
no-one else embraced me
with that

Year 67

Bird Throng

fluttering wings bring them
quickly dipping
to the curved arms of the stand
they study the feeders
pick out safe landings
execute a swift foray
zigzag off over roof-tops

I smile at their antics
their aerobatic dexterity
their petty squabbles

pleased my generosity
has brought happiness
I relax in the lounger
forget that this entertainment
is their day's work

dancing flight not for joy
to protect from predators
the perch atop the pole
to check for risk
that speedy departure
is not for fun—

                this is survival

Year 2

Worm

once I ate a worm
didn't do any harm
didn't taste very nice
won't eat a worm twice

Year 55

mining silver coins on Coniston

Coniston reflects a dance of silver coins from its hammered surface, an arts and crafts view. I watch red sails, a romantic Arthur Ransom movement, slowly passing, a ketch to carry me on its careful passage into the past, quietly confirming why this view talks of ships and sealing wax, of cabbages and poetry, on this madding June day. I would worship dale and mist, dream, and the hope of dreams, breathe the day-hot air, that tranquil space between lake and evening, breathe out, savour the departing breath, how good it feels, how meant

Year 8

No blue plaque

the paper shop beside
Iceland's car park
where I was served by the hand
that held the ball that twisted
batsmen into noughts

the cricket field gates
how often did I wait
to see him enter for
the game all ready
in his whites

the house beside
the ground so close
he changed at home
from grey gardener
to super- hero

the clock above
the pavilion roof
they say he hit it
with a six or two
before my time

Year 72

Desiderata—out of Covid desolation

Build and pull down until there is perfection, or as near it as you can achieve in your allotted time. Let life be a journey to the end, where vision meets reality and death is an acceptance of achieving what was begun, to the satisfaction of those left. Let us remember the sacrifices of others, the world is a better place for the lives of many, the things given not thrown away, not a closed tightness but in the open spaces. Always see beyond self to the opportunity, to that space, the future - for life is finite but possibility is endless.

Can you hear above the roar of progress, the cars, the planes, the chattering shoppers, the televisions, there is an ant walking?

Stop, there is more to be seen than you take time to discover.

Suddenly, the taste of life will be sweet when you seize those moments to enjoy it.. There are new sensations to place upon your tongue. Depend on your inner being, unfetter your senses, forget what is acceptable and do what needs to be done. Make a place where you are at peace, and all who you meet there may feel contented, and will leave refreshed, and in this place accept your failings and successes with equanimity, for both are you, the likeable motive and what is envious and devious, remember both, undo what is bitter.

Be still, be still – ambition will not find better, merely other.

Year 72

When Edison found light

it was one of those moment
drunk   party hats   on empty heads
and a fire not in a fireplace or pit or
anywhere you would put a fire
an accidental burning of his house
so there were these fried fish
not in batter   but he had vinegar
he knew that   but couldn't find it
so he tipped the fish into a bowl
poured paraffin on instead – seemed
a good idea   as most drunk thoughts
are not when you are sober   but
drunk are brilliant   and this was
so brilliant   have you seen
a burning carp   it flares especially
those waving fins – so he had a thought
another   he was full
of them that day   threw the bowl
over the fish   and suddenly
all was flame   and bright   and sight
a light in a bowl   and he hung it high
saw how like an upside-down onion
how it was a bulb   and shouted
to his drunk companions   see
I had that light-bulb moment
this they agreed   phoned   well
once one of them invented the phone
phoned the Patent office   said
Mr Edison has an idea

Year 7

My Earth is Flat

Seen through Mercator's Projection
I did not recognise the distortion
of distance and time. Reality flattened.
In the centre was Britain,
East and West defined by zero meridian,
countries pushed to the edge.

Being flat, my world fitted on school walls,
decorated corridors and infant class-rooms.
Pink of British Empire stood out,
like an incomplete jigsaw, waiting
for another piece claimed by a Clive or Biggles,
conversion of the barbarians; Civilisation.

Though the oceans were in pale blue,
I knew it was untrue,
for Britannia ruled the waves,
our gunboats diplomatically reminding,
every sea should be tinted with a faint pink,
a wash covering the globe.

The old school building has been raised to the ground.
The Empire has crumbled to the Commonwealth.
The waters of the world no longer bloodied,
but I still see Britain at the centre,
pull apart the globe,
measure the earth as if time stopped
         at Greenwich.

Year 25

Thoughts on a brown gown

it was not how she saw herself
not how she was

yet it was how I saw her
still see her
forty-five years on

- long dress with side split
letting her leg shine against silk
deep dark brown

no pattern or adornment
plunging neckline tantalising
beauty teased

her mother
barely glanced at the dress
dismissed for the classic gown
high necked blue which suited her eyes

and she was beautiful in blue
but I wanted her daring
to stun the room

it is how I remember
her lithe and young and glowing
in brown

Year 46

Out-going tide

I linger at the rock pool,
step back into childhood.
The day changes overhead
warm then cold on my bent back.

The view alters with the sky;
reflections shut me out,
until shadows skid across
reopening the scenes below.

Bright red anemones at the waterline,
a crab, size of a finger-nail, scuttles,
pincers pull at shreds of sea-weed
as water-boatmen skim above.

A sea-breeze creases between the rocks,
whispering old names, talking of Arran,
Bute, Cumbrae, Ailsa Craig
summers on the Clyde.

The thrum of a diesel engine,
the sharp cry of gulls trailing astern,
pulls me from the enclosed space,
eyes lifted to the beach,

draped with a necklace of seaweed,
bejewelled with shiny cans,
trimmed with plastic.

Year 33

To Sail Away

He built his boat
every summer
sheets of ply nailed and glued
a hotch-potch of surfaces and angles

After three years
it resembled a catamaran
floated
nearly level

He could not bend plywood so
it was shaped like a miniature stealth-ship
a tiny vessel for a small wiry man
as if he wanted to sail away
slip out under the radar

At low tide on the harbour mud
he painted the bottom red, the rest white
carefully picked out details in black

One day he erected a short mast
mounted a small out-board on the stern
phut-phut-phutted round the harbour

He moored it on a long rope from the quayside
so that it rose and fell with the tides
the only movement it made from that day on
until pulled ashore the following summer

Its twin hulls with blunt bow and flat stern
like red and white coffins on the slipway
holding a dead-man's dreams

Year 3

A tortoise in a Parliament

bright the day the pavement warm
the street is empty and the gate
is dad's embracing green
matching our front door

my pedal trike is red and yellow
my fun is pottering in nothing
just me and smiles
the challenge of pedals

but on the hill a cloud
gathers somehow threatens
though the day has not changed
and laughter echoes from afar

the swoop of crows the pecking
the stab of beaks and piercing tongues
how much blood can a child spill
how good are tears for blunting knives

their blows sound on my shell
a slow withdrawal
into my own world
another burden on my back

Year 30

Worship in the Tabernacle—Corrie

for Joan Eardley

Here on the shore of Corrie   she started her journey.
Joan and Margot Sandeman   sharing   the Tabernacle,
one bedroom and a tiny studio   opened to   the Firth,
the weather and the light. Here on the shore   at Corrie
looking   along the gorse, a splash of blue   suggests
boat, her vision   She wrote to Margot   yesterday
I was painting a fir tree in the Castle Wood   when the
deluge came   suddenly   I would not be beaten   again
by the blasted rain   Decided not to give in   I made
a tent   from my raincoat   your old bicycle   and ropes.
It must have looked funny   to people   from the road.
Joan learned to thole it would lash herself to the easel.
A beginning to all those journeys   to Catterline   where
the storms   could rage   around her   where she could
strap herself to the canvas.   At Corrie a child saw her
came up to this woman   in baggy trousers   looking so
poor and offered her his coppers   did she take away
to the children in Glasgow   the openness of the child
catch   the honesty   of the face   capture it   in colours
in the same way she grabbed   the truth of storm   gale
sun   rain   cloud   field   cottage   belonging

Year 71

On the Final Journey of Wise Men

There are seven now for the others burnt out
in the long push through this desert
when they said Global Warming
that the Gulf Stream would turn fickle
head to the Arctic and melt   seas would flood
low lying settlements half a continent
we content in our city certainty believed nothing
would come to this
it was not floods that swamped the street choked
air-con fans   strangled cars   derailed our trains
from the West came winds hot miserable
old images of farmers in Thirties dust-bowl haunted
our packing our departure heading South
East   Europe   Asia   Australia   Antarctica
anywhere but here
we have travelled broken places without comfort
but there was no anywhere   there was only need
to come home
trudge our sand drowned city
in sunset haze we near shelter
ahead the Flat Iron Building's prow breaks the dunes
and we are without tears   or hope

Year 30

Condemned by beauty

cut flowers from cellophane, slice the rubber band which ties and arrange, ready them for death, for their suffering, watch them droop and hang, fading, dying, smile as they die, say it brings life into the house, glory of nature, how the colours sing in the vases, cut crystal tombs, art glass fashioned to commemorate the sacrifice, a galaxy of daffodil to herald spring, how bright the yellow trumpets of requiem, in forecourt and supermarket, in florist and market stall, wreaths of the dying to celebrate, birthdays, weddings, to seduce, darling, I have slaughtered twelve blood-red roses, this is love, is joy, in the hearse lie white lilies of the dead, another illegitimacy, their day in the fields denied, not for them to be wind tossed, sing in rain, faces no longer to follow the sun, in artificial light, central heated limbo, stems suck for dregs of life, bright clad prisoners parched on windowsill, scorched in conservatory, abandoned in the unused room, condemned by beauty

Year 48

Bamburgh Castle

1

Stone and rock as one climb
from the village cricket pitch, ringed by memorial benches
from which to contemplate its mass.

On the outfield a marquee awaits the bride,
bedecked guests scatter over the green
until summoned by the echoing hooves of two black horses
bringing the wedding party from the church.

When dusk grasps at the castle, floodlights reveal
fresh shadow and mystery.
Evening dog walkers, strolling couples, children stretching the day
catch glimpses through the marquee flap of the dancers
casting images on the canvas walls.

2

On the road from Seahouses,
black shadowed buttresses of rock and stone thrust battlements into
the blue.
then hidden by dunes, until the signs for car-parks
and the castle reappears.

Behind the castle lies the beach where sand slips
into the North Sea and the sea glides into the horizon,
barely interrupted by the Farne Islands,
with their seabird colonies and breeding grey seals,
pulling daytime cruises from Seahouses.

On those boats I have watched
the puffins wave hop,
grimaced at the smell of bird colonies,
even more at the annoyance of strangers,
while wondering if guillemots, in the squabbles on the cliffs,
look on neighbours with similar disgust and desire
to drown among the bobbing seals.

3

On the beach beneath the castle I avoid the crowds,
walk in the early morning or in the peace of evening
through miniature sandstorms sweeping from water's edge
to marram grass holding captive the restless sand.
Listen to the chatter of the wavelets, the call of seagulls,
feel the weight of the castle pressing on its rock,
experience the push and pull, lift and drop, of timeless forces.

The Castle, the village, the beach, like some private gravity
pulling me back in reality and memory.

4

I watch for Bamburgh Castle from the A1
it beckons over fields of corn
the castle a flat grey outline.

Turn at the filling station at Purdy Lodge,
take the bends at Lucker,
bounce on the level-crossing, after waiting
as the London Express rocks the car,
on past unpronounceable Glororum.

Eyes stray from the road to the red stone of the castle,
meeting the memories leaping from the ramparts
to dance on the cricket pitch or stroll the beach.

When I am dead surely a part of me will be here
drifting in the haar,
until the castle becomes a trace of red sand,
the village dark patterns on fallow land,
the cricket pitch a blaze of wild flowers.

The sea will still glide into the sky
on the Farnes birds crying above grey seals
on an empty wave

Year 72

As if

and I remember Brigflatts
how the spirit of contentment
seeps from wall and pew
The Meeting Hall like a life boat
arriving in a swelling gale
so salvation seems possible

and I remember a Welsh Chapel
with ancient holy spring
and inside it a gate
to hold the shepherd's dogs
as if Come-by and away
would herd me into safety

and I remember Notre Dame
settling its breath upon me
choir voices clear and crisp
as if angels came to me singing
as if there was a heaven
as if I might kiss my dead

Year 11

Nothing but a paper pusher

I linger in streets
not discretely
I shout unintelligible phrases
to the addicted
late night seekers
who need the latest buzz
push money in my hand
slink away head bowed
in speedy digestion
I wave temptation
in the face of another punter
-- the city's evening news
a paper pusher

Year 57

Plasticine to Camembert

Said plasticine to camembert
I feel like brie I could be brie
why do people not compare
said plasticine to camembert
It will look like me just wait and see
when mucky fingers pull it free
Said plasticine to camembert
I feel like brie I could be brie

Year 19

Pub Faces—In All Her Glory

It is not
her face that
swings into view
though it is a pleasant
face young and plump ripe
and happily sharing happiness
as she curves her way to the table
the friend beside her is a 'looker' taller
slimmer sways in harmony but tonight the gaze
    is pulled to her pale skin caressed
        by the black top plunging
            beyond daring

Year 27

Please mind the gap

I try to protect it
for it must be delicate
I am exhorted in every station
to Mind the Gap

I leap forward as the train stops
stand guard   protective
as it shakes in diesel nervousness

but there is a shrill whistle
and it is gone
one moment there then
nothing

every stop and start
a gap is born and dies
I cannot save it

am left forlorn
having failed
again

Year 10

Nancy Pretty

the small garden at the side of my childhood home
was split into beds each bordered by flowers
a neat row of pink and white stars
Nancy Pretty
they were called Nancy Pretty
and I would never pick them or cross over them
or stand on them even though the paths were narrow
and I was young and reckless
my mother's name was Nancy
and I believed these were my father's way of saying
that he loved her
this line of tiny, perpetual, flowers in summer
showing his love
not showy or loud, delicate and beautiful
and I felt safe
held in those borders

Year 57

At Moniack—this landscape has not changed

Midnight and alone I sit
in the Hobbit House at Moniack
trying to trap thoughts in a feeble net
mouthing prayers for the past
looking out to a framed sky

pinprick lights say cottage farm
late night traveller
full moon painting all with silver
a glow that lets the eye catch
distant mountains the valley floor

dark arms of Scots Pine point east
and west
saying there are other lands unknown
misunderstood
where the sun is yet to die
where rain will not fall tomorrow

and I
think only pine and hill
only bus and bus
back to the comfort of home.

Year 22

A Law unto Himself

he clothes in a mirror of himself
an external reflection of who he
wants to be seen to be

but not him
not how he would dress
for comfort or by choice

these covers are expected
no bright colours or flamboyancy
no fancy trim

he is staid
businessman in career suit
black tilted hat of dour aspect

no-one expects the red dress
high heels and sparkling fascinator
in his wardrobe

that he dons at night
to wander his dark corners

Year 66

Agnes Burns—Song Book

in these sheets are her memories
valued so much she had them bound
her name placed on the cover

think of the cost of each sheet
the care to collect and have them fixed in time
torn pages repaired with lines of stitches

these sheets hold her memories
the nights by candle light
times of harmony with brother   mother   sister
friends gathered to share the rhythm of life
love and loss   celebration and sadness

these sheets hold her memories and
our imagination of her and her brother
we mingle our voice with dead choirs
words living in the beat   note by note
we hope to gather them to us
sit by a smoky fire
merge today and yesterday

these sheets hold her and us
song much more than words and music
song like the clear spring   cold on the tongue
tastes of nothing and everything
brings us laughing from the well
somehow more alive

Year 22

Into Heaven

What happened then
when you surrendered
your body as a sacrifice
trusting I would take it
worshipping

What altar was laid out with candlestick
proud standing burning symbol of my hopes
to have you lay
your alabaster skin upon the sheet
and offer it to me

What ancient wells were tasted
what sacred runes explored
my fingers tracing each curve
uncovering the timeless mysteries

What doubts that all is but
another ritual of a feeble mind
These Gods are liars or were never there
and yet the certainty prevails
that we have entered into Heaven

Year 54

Edge of time

I knew a man who said, he would not be missed,
but I could not forget, the way that it was said,
and so I went again, to where he used to sit,
upon the edge of time.

Others saw me there, searching in that place,
and asked me why I looked, so lost and in despair.
I told them, that in truth, I did not understand,
but felt I had to speak to the man who I had seen
upon the edge of time.

They asked me for my name and nodded when I said.
They expected me to come and were told that they must say,
that he was here but now had gone away,
that I should take his place and wait for my day too,
upon the edge of time.

They left me there alone, in emptiness and grief,
as he would never know that I remembered him,
and as I thought of this, a man approaching stopped,
upon the edge of time.

Leaping to my mouth, came that phrase, which haunted me.
I placed my hand on him, and whispered in his ear,
you are young and you are bold, go and carve your name,
I stay sitting here, until I disappear, and I will not be missed
upon the edge of time.

The young man turned and went, indeed why would he stay,
but I could see, within, my words were haunting him
and he would not forget, the way that they were said,
and so would come again, to this place where I did sit
upon the edge of time.

I stepped into the dark, shouting as I went,
one day there will be found, an old man searching here,
ask him for his name, and no matter his reply,
tell him I was here and now have gone away,
and he must settle here, to one day understand,
upon the edge of time.

Year 23

Drive a Hillman Imp and you'll want to smile

Drive a Hillman Imp if you want to smile
its engine singing to your laughing heart.
Car and you as one, joy in every mile
drive a Hillman Imp if you want to smile.
The style, that look, it was a car apart
from the rest, classic automotive art.
Drive a Hillman Imp and you'll want to smile
its engine singing with your happy heart.

Year 68

For Tammy and Robert—Wedding At Sherbrooke Castle Hotel

if this room had hips they would be swaying
Sherbrooke Castle Hotel jitterbugging down Nithsdale Road
today is love distilled elixir of life flowing
all round are electric smiles
web of family and friends
each silken thread gleaming
embraces bride and groom
love knot pulled ever tighter

Year 9

Old Mrs Kerr

in the tenement where I first learned
the fragility of buildings the foolishness of men
how if you pull down a wall without plan
do not put in any new support a building breaks
floors slope walls crack

I return to how sun fractured the bay
how deep blue the Clyde could be
how cold Oh how cold
and feel again a summer day's disappointment
when dragged from sun-warm sand to
the dark nest of our hostess

Now I long for that cool darkness
the birdlike lady who fluttered among
dark brocade high backed chairs
a plethora of ornaments
the table ready with frightening delicate china
so dainty even tiny fingers did not fit these handles

the tea poured through silver strainer
the sugar bowl with neat cubes and the tongs
slipping in fingers the dread splash as the dropped
cube shattered surface tension

How Mrs Kerr smiled and chatted and laughed
and busied with choices of new baked scones
Danish fancies pancakes sponges sitting proudly
on the cake stand which politeness said had not
to be touched but to wait until offered

and there beside the theatre glasses for watching
the vessels going to and from Glasgow docks
her lace-maker's pad Mum asks her to show
how lace is made and those old fingers deftly
lift and lay bobbins spinning their web of leaves
with pattern appearing roses and vines the spread
bobbins threads woven round the pins and she
so casual about her craft visible in the napkins
antimacassars in the collar of her black dress

fading into mist and tears for all those dead holidays
the buried love the frittered frittered

Year 51

Although that love was mine

I never knew who you were
never gave you any time
too tied up in my desires
as long as I was fine
I never truly saw your love
although that love was mine

In looking back I realise
how little I discovered
of how you thought and how you felt
the world that you encountered
for in myself I lived each day
no other truth uncovered

I did not stop to look at you
as years brought grey and deeper line
and in my need I failed to know
the person hidden in each sign
I did not understand your love
although that love was mine

Year 52

Blackbird in the Holly

Where once the early blackbird made her nest
and mother called me urgent in for tea
now is a paradise long lost to me
hopes shattered like the egg I carried home

I try to catch a happiness in flight
but as with sunlight fallen in the leaves
the slightest breeze changing light and shade
the mystery is where and how to seize

for moments it is there then it is dead
the fledgling breath snuffed out, a merest puff
the secret wishes made in former days
are lately hidden in the holly bush

Life has flown and left an empty shell
the dandelion no-longer holds my dreams
that childhood clock laid bare, blown away
and I no-longer hear my mother call.

Year 18

Right Up Tight

A touch of silk
or a shimmer of satin, grey seduction
strut and pose
redefined masculinity
contained in a rib-boned package
bound by thongs of black and red

Life's a picnic
laze on a summer's afternoon
cotton discarded
briefly surrender
to a slinkier touch, a frivolous desire
drop convention in a flash of pink

pull on the frilly nylon knickers

Year 68

Song for lost windows

somewhere there is glass
somewhere framed opportunity
a landscape of futures
horizons and mountains
places sunlit joyous young
lovers to wander
dreamers to explore

somewhere they open
let in hope let out singing

somewhere beyond these shutters
barriered and bolted
painted black
behind these walls
bricked up plastered
is where I used to lust
believe the outside lived

how is it I have burrowed in years
buried away
lie broken shattered
without windows

Year 72

Playing with Truth

The board has lost its shape
the tidy pattern   I once believed
like 3-d chess   a nightmare of levels
pieces jambed into holes
a hasty travel-game saved and in
disarray

Truth is grinning   self-satisfaction
the liar who said there were rules
I rewrite them daily   as Truth suggests
as if I understood

my chessmen lie in broken formation
I mould an army of pawns   more
than needed   yet less   as if
quantity carried any virtue

sails billow   I am at sea
no longer solid   underfoot
the shifting   shifting   of the shifting
horizon bent and Newton has his rainbow
depending on where you are   looking
if I close my eyes I will not be blind
but sightless   nothing is black or white
so grey meets Truth dressed in grey

death is true
dark at my side   will never fail   me

truth is laughing
sees my sea lying   storm   blown
wanderings must come to harbour
every pigeon roosts

Truth dismembers my pieces
like the fox in the dovecot
droppings unpicked from my labours

my rooks are embattled
my white Knights devious   unseated by

a Sicilian Defence   a wing gambit
my bishops opened mouthed cursing

if this is true water of life
why am I drowning

Truth turns three cards
can I believe

Year 61

When the trees move

there is that bastard thing   of breathing
the effort of filling and exhale
how conscious are the walls   of pressure
changes in the passage of air
just once I would like not to hear
not to feel   I will realise
death has come   gentle and welcome
and the squabble of sparrows   refilling
of the feeder   falls to someone else
tomorrow   let the wind pass through
the ashes of a fire   neighbours whisper
I wonder who we will get

Year 57

Lindisfarne

In the footsteps of monks, I walk
wet sand like a grey mirror
sliding into a grey sea, which drifts
into a blue-grey sky.

The low dunes stand watchful guardians
of this vaulted peace

Ahead two bodies, one a reflection,
foetal, hooded, imagined reality, I know
cannot be true

They are an illusion, formed by the brokenness
of a tree washed bare, reclothed in green and brown
by the sea, shades of life in death.

On this half-bright day, I wander
the margins of Lindisfarne
exposed, as the tide ebbs and flows,
boundaries changing.

Year 50

The Question is...

The question is not how I am but who? Whether it is important to know if the I of Me is in the eye of you. I have a vision in the physical but also in my head. Fragments of memory, lingering, a taste in my mouth, a tingle in my feet, a chill; these will not matter. There are pieces of me left in rooms and with people; these are impressions made in soil where I have stood, in hearts where I have intruded. I feel the silk of a breast, the warmth of sun, waves, there are always waves, breaking, on rocks, breaking on me. Rough pebbles, sand in toes, grit on the streets, blowing in my eyes, and I hear the roar of engines, the hiss of steam from trains—my mother calling me home. I would go to be held. Have Dad lay his hand on my back, say well done. In a crowded room there are smiles of welcome. They shout my name and suddenly there is an I who exists beyond Me; an I who is a stranger and greeted with generosity. I am surprised.

I cannot save happiness. There is no bank, no vault in which to lock the moment. There are residues to be mined but after the slag has been discarded, it is always less, less than the feeling of joy, only a knowledge of its loss. We might never experience happiness again, that is the horror. The dark tunnels inhabited where past terrors arrive, more powerful with each incarnation, and those candles of hope flicker and burn out. I gather wax remnants, melt, pour round a wick, but cannot save the scent of almonds, of dates.

Year 54

Miles to go before we sleep

after Robert Frost

We started with the killing   so thoughtless   so casual   broken death lies in the hollow places   in the bones scattered   in the hidden dips   where the air is dank   sunlight never enters where it is hard to find the debris Gather every iota of what was search diligently in the glaur   and gore of death   Make a drawing of where they are found   list where they would have been when living   plan plan plan   This is not the work of an instant but it must be done   There is a lifetime's destruction   be prepared to spend a lifetime rebuilding The skeleton of resurrection is a work of love   not to be undertaken lightly   or on a whim   Believe in it and in you   link piece by piece   until the body reappears   the weight on our hearts is that we find there is still the missing   we must remember what was   We must remember what was lost   We must tell of it   There are ways to balance   need   desire hope   we must find the point   where we embrace   give all things their place   in dark times   find   what we believe hold it   no matter the distractions   the threats   Be true to self is not a cliché   This is the resistance   we have to find so that tomorrow's children have their opportunity to struggle on Do not inherit a wasteland   What was given to us must be theirs and more   more   more

Year 9

Standing Stones, Kingarth, Isle of Bute

I run ahead to the standing stones
hidden in the wood
enticed by a desire to jump out
frighten the others

I will reappear
like a ghost or a sprite
a creature of the dark spaces

when I arrive alone
tree ranks turn black
in the gloaming

an absence of bird song
only the dry twisting of branches
wind-shifted needles

sudden cold creeps up
I shiver in fear

stones change grey shapes
trees lean in to stare down
I crouch in a malevolent dream

forest no longer a playground
friendly welcome pine-fresh
now an ancient primal place

I feel a presence that is
not human an unreal other
as I wait for family

they cannot be more
than minutes away
I hear their safety

but the path becomes timeless
their voices echo and fade
are never nearer

I am held here

frozen in longing
for mother father brothers

rooted to this spot
by incantation of tree and wind
I belong to the stones

Year 72

all the dogs died

he trapped sprites on the hillside
with light   and spell
discovered they were better than collies

faster over the ground
walls   fences   as if never there
in a way they were not
passing straight through
a flash   puff of energy
out the other side

cum bye   away lass
he kept the old commandments
though lie down seemed foolish
more hover   but it carried
across moorland   and valley
the sharp crack of his voice

stinging like his eyes
when he saw fairies in the mirror
over the hearth   at night
remembered when the dogs lay by the fire
patiently   waiting   tails twitching
when he spoke   or a car came

there were no cars now
no dogs for sale

how long before the sheep vanished
the horses came   were gone
nothing was the same

Year 5

Glacé Fruits

Every year it arrived late,
the Christmas box from South Africa,
the fruits sealed in sugar,
slices of orange and peach,
the grapes and plums,
preserved, so that we could indulge,
and I hesitated, fingers twitching.
Choice was glorious luxury
in a time of rationing.

One New Year,
the railwayman, who had emigrated,
brought the box with him.
He told of the servants,
the boy who worked the garden,
the girl who served at table,
but they had no worth in his new world.
In mine they were waifs,
but somehow I knew
his dismissal of them meant
he was a smaller man than
the child who heard him,
his disconnection from reality,

but I still ate the fruit,
anticipated the parcel.

Year 53

This door is not a means of escape

Royal Alexandra Hospital

Doors open
access to another place

or close
isolate

offer a choice
you twist

but you do not read
the warning

in panic
exit
to nowhere

wait

Year 16

Holiday Slides

this is Mary and I
Geneva near the lake
we're in front of the bus

this is Mary and I
Lucerne near the lake
in front of the bus
the man in between is our driver
Billy

this is Billy and Mary Tom and Louise
the bus is in the hotel carpark
just out of sight is...
Mary what was that mountain?

This is me and Louise
in front of the bus in the Hotel carpark
a marvellous view of the Rhine valley
to our left

this is Mary and I
in front of the bus
that street in Glasgow near the Cathedral
saying good-bye to Billy

Year 6

Walking toy

Body
of pink
and white
the cow has
angled feet so
that it rocks when
tapped on its flanks
as long as the prod is
gentle   almost unfelt
when   the surface slopes
gravity takes the raised legs
on one side of the happy body
to swing forward slowly change
the balance   extended feet   now
heavier   so the cow sways   tilts
to that side   and rocks on   sedately
or trots if the slope is increased   races
madly if taken to   extremes   tapping
and   rocking until it falls over or drops
                                            off
                                                the
                                                end

inevitably
even   simple
mechanisms fail
there   comes   a day
a pair of legs   snaps
too many times break-leg
speed   too   many   crashes
and   a child   learns   that life
is   fun   laughter   and   an ever
changing   slide   to   destruct
                                      i
                                     o
                                  n

a child's
simple   fun
lesson in rules
of living   control
of slope   of speed
             destruction
                    never belongs
                            to
                             the
                              t
                               o
                               y

Year 24

Black Park, Tullochgrue

brimmin wi howps
an couthie wi plichtit trowth
yer answer maks ma heart sae fu

aye lassie we dinna ken
whit lies aheid
nor daed we fash

thegither we'd meet sang an sair
thon lang road wis diamond sealed
naething wis dauntin

sae we steppit oot
prood wis a tae hae ye
in aside

mony years lang syne
mony lauchs mony greets
an am mair stentit

there's nane can doot, I'd the braw
pairt o oor deal
A widna change a meenit

A micht hae chosen mair romantic
tae start oot frae than a Black Park
we dinnae like tae tell the hale jing-bang

we'd lauch aboot it on oor ain
sayin it doesnae maiter whaur it stairtit
it's whaur it gaes

Year 66

hopeful of words

I hesitate at my desk   hopeful of words
hopeful   of a white page   and black ink
of the multicoloured books   which line
the shelves   so many   closed   pages
of words   waiting to be drained   to slake
my thirst   there is a whiff of panic   in
their stale dust covers   which cry out
I am here for you   and you alone bring
me life   so live   find me   open and read
your future   your past   your living   and
your dead   and I do not want to leave
until I discover if   they lie

outside my window   this day   is dull
the bird-feeder   is alive   with sparrows
my waited throng   my choir   of choice
my garden   flutters   with angel wings
dashing from hedge to feeder   a delight
of chirping   a memory   of country lane
leading back to a distant town   on Arran
childish delight   in Firth   and mountain
a pirate yacht   stealing   my boyish heart
as it sailed   to the horizon   carrying
an unknown dream

Year 9

Meditation on Kirkwall

From the tower of St Magnus Cathedral
   looking down on the chancel roof

        feel
     a suction
    a desire to flip
   into the void to break
  the link between feet and
ground to fall
                        fall
                              fall
                                   f

                                   a

                                   l

                                   l

Year 59

Thoughts in a spring garden

The garden once again
is turning fresher green, and buds
peek out.   Dark winter plods
away and spring applauds the songs
as early day belongs
to the fresh mating throngs.   So too
I find a smile breaks through
For who would remain blue in sight
of all in warm sunlight.
Depression; put to flight; Black slain.

Year 63

Home to Orkney

I leave home, walk down my street in Paisley,
wondering how it will go. Am I crazy
to think that I will reconnect the child
who, fifty or more years ago, was thrilled
by an Orkney sea and sky, and so my
memories are azure tinted   and I ,
the cynic, have given this journey such weight
each footstep echoes 'you are tempting fate,
and to those echoes 'you are tempting fate'
rush for a dark blue bus, dread being late.
I awoke hours before the alarm was set
I have skipped breakfast, no drinks, for toilets
or lack of them looms, demands abstinence.
Relax.   I want this experience to be intense.

(kp) {x} \n (pk) {x} \n {y}

rumbling wheels
support the stuffed case
a mind overflowing

(kp) {x} \n (pk) {x} \n {y}

My route to Glasgow is well known, so I
can relax. A child boards, catches my eye,
smiles that open welcome. The pale-blue gaze
lights an already laughing day, and he says,
to his mother, 'Sit here'. 'Sit here. The high
seat by the door.' He climbs, as mother sighs,
to be above, to command his view of
the passing world, which flickers on and off,
for tenements cast shadows, which do not
cloud his life; or mine. Child father of the thought
that this journey will go well, and is not
something to regret. All my doubts forgotten. Comforted, I reach Buchanan Street.
Toilet 30 pence, you're joking, I can wait.

(kp) {x} \n (pk) {x} \n {y}

Journey begun
the case seems lighter
hopes rolling

(kp) {x} \n (pk) {x} \n {y}

A girl, brighter than this day, asks me
'Is this the stance for Inverness?' Smiles, she
sits beside me and we chat, in fact she
is also going to Orkney, home from Uni,
just graduated in textile design at
Galashields. Is hoping to work at
fashion design in Glasgow, or London.
Our bus, again in blue livery, drives in.
I take the seat behind her on the bus,
leave space beside her for her bags, and thus
we travel. At Perth we change bus, onward
I read poetry by Alice Oswald,
on my Kobo.   I do the *Herald*
puzzles, first sudoku and then the crossword.

(kp) {x} \n (pk) {x} \n {y}

A9- No problem
with no wheel to hold
blue sky thinking

(kp) {x} \n (pk) {x} \n {y}

Arrival Inverness, 20 minutes late,
choice is to get food or to urinate.
Food wins. Eaten by the shelter as it
rains. I watch the girl's bag for her toilet
break.   The rain is heavier. Our bus pulls in

blue, white, yellow of a summer day, thin
water seeping round my shoes, turning jacket
darker, as I make certain my case gets
loaded.   I settle by a window near
the back, I have seldom been north from here
and take in everything as we head for Tain.
Blue sky returning, we outrun the rain.
Up past Golspie, wrong side for the statue.
Dunrobin. I wonder if that is true

(kp){x}\n(pk){x}\n{y}

Truth and lies
cases roll on beyond
one lifetime

(kp) {x} \n (pk) {x} \n {y}

Now doubts return.   That niggard drunk nibbles at
my soul, like some late-night battered fish pulled at
carelessly. We shall miss my Hamnavoe
connection and then I will have to go
to a lonely B&B. Dreaming
of the places I have dreamt of re-seeding,

nightmare of broken strands, broken me, broken

The flag-stone fences ring in this imposter
as driver picks up the pace. Disaster
may be avoided. Marielle, the friendly
girl has a name, Marielle, said briefly
as we boarded, we should be alright for
time. I curse every passenger for
any destination other than my own
Relax. Sit quiet.   Orkney will not die unknown

(kp){x}\n(pk){x}\n{y}

Life rolls on
Wheels spinning unbidden
The thread

(kp){x}\n(pk){x}\n{y}

An Orkney sea an Orkney sky and I
together
lie at harbour.

I travelled 14 hours
The thread of road weaving north

The textile printed, years ago,
reclothes

I wrap myself in.

(kp){x}\n(pk){x}\n{y}

Unburdened
the case empty
a mind at rest

Year 71

Here in the poets zoo

if you sit with me
quietly in the shadows
you can avoid being blinded
by the stellar quines
glorious Eliots
a-strutting their peacock words

creep between their sheets
hear egos mating
please keep silent
when they produce
another haibun
or low doggerel

these were once endangered
hid away in dank crevices
in the corners of bars
in the charity of church halls

now see how they flourish
brought out by the rap of glasses
on well-heeled boots
they have grown bold

if they see you are interested
they will descend like vampires
to suck out your thoughts
string them onto lines
wave them triumphant

shouting I have found

A POEM